Suffolk-Punch
"The Gentle Giant"
For Kids

Nature Books for Kids
By
K. Bennett

Mendon Cottage Books

JD-Biz Publishing

Read More Amazing Animal Books

Purchase at Amazon.com

Table of Contents

Introduction

"Majestic. Calm temperament. Hard worker. Beautiful. Energetic. Willing to serve."

***

The Suffolk Punch is an amazing horse with kind eyes and a willing spirit. However, unlike other horses, it is not well known. Have you ever heard of the Suffolk Punch before? Maybe not!

This beautiful horse goes by many names like Suffolk Horse and Suffolk Sorrel. As a draft horse, they are tall, strong, and have a beautiful Chestnut coat. But the spelling of the color is different than you might think. Instead of Chestnut, it is spelled CHESNUT with a missing letter T. So, the color is Chesnut and not chestnut!

As mentioned, the Suffolk Punch is a ***draft horse.*** This is a horse that "draws" or "hauls" something. It is also called a work horse or heavy horse, because it works hard and pulls heavy loads. However, these types of horses are strong, docile, easy to work with and very patient.

The more recent history of the Suffolk Punch goes back many years to World War I. During those years, this horse became a work horse on big farms. One reason why farmers liked this horse so much was because of its personality. Their calm and patient nature was exactly what farmers needed to help them work better. Farmers also loved this horse because they are hard workers!

What else can we learn about them?

The Suffolk Punch gets its name from the country of Suffolk. And Punch was added because of how of strong it is! These horses have a good walk or gait, high energy and a unique color.

However, some horse owners use creative names to call their horses by other labels. For example some say: dull dark, red, bright and dark liver.

Apart from the beautiful color, the Suffolk Punch has a beautiful, white star on the forehead or blaze down the front of their face.

What makes this horse unique?

Today, Suffolk Punch horses are used in forestry, advertising and for pleasure driving. With their loving personality, gentle nature and big heart, the Suffolk Punch is a great horse and a fun animal to learn about!

Remember: Every single creature on this diverse planet can teach us something wonderful. So take a few minutes to learn about these noble creatures that have captured our imagination, our minds and our hearts!

Suffolk Punch

Chapter 1

Taking a stroll in the field

History: In 1586, an English historian known as William Camden published a book entitled *Britannia*. In this book, he described a horse with the characteristics of the Suffolk Punch. This was the first time many people heard about this noble horse.

The ancestors of this lovable horse are called Fell and Dales. These are British ponies. The Suffolk Punch is also related to the Haflinger. If you have never heard these names before…just keep on reading!

Fell: This Pony is very beautiful. They are highly intelligent, lively and alert. They are also part of the working breed of ponies from the North of England, Westmorland and Northumberland. (If you do not recognize these names or are curious, ask your parent or a guardian to help you find the locations on a map)

Dales: These ponies are strong, sturdy, intelligent and friendly. Their name comes from the Dales region of England. This is also a working breed and was used for many tasks during the war.

Haflinger: These horses are small but elegant. Their ancestry is very old, all the way back to the middle ages. But they have a lot of energy, a smooth walk or gait and were very versatile.

As mentioned before, the Suffolk Punch gets a lot of characteristics from these horses! For this reason, many farmers used this breed for farm work and rarely sold them. They were more of a member of the family.

These noble horses also pulled ploughs and carried the wheat to the mill so the town could eat. This included farm machinery, non-motorized vans and buses, which simple means people had no engines for their vehicles, except for the horses!

Do you know what a *plough* is? You probably know a farmer has to plant things. A farmer has to get the seeds into the ground and cover them with enough dirt; In this case a plough is a handy instrument to use. Why? Did you ever try to plant something with just your hands? Is it easy or hard to do? This is one reason why farmers use a plough. It makes their job a lot easier.

This machine prepares or loosens the soil to plant the seeds. When the plough goes through the dirt, important nutrients are brought to the surface and these nutrients are important for the seeds to grow healthy and strong. Today, this type of machine will be pulled by a tractor but in the past, horses were used like the Suffolk Punch.

Sadly, as the years went by, this beautiful breed lost a lot of horses, not only because of the war but also because of better farming methods that didn't use horses anymore.

Today, this breed is considered "critical," because in 2007 the Suffolk Horse Society recorded 36 pure bred foals. That's not much, right?

Happily, many people are trying to save this amazing animal. And because of this, these horses are slowly increasing. Isn't that wonderful?

FUN FACTS FOR KIDS: What is HANDS?

This is a neat way to measure horses. The measurement refers to hands, literal hands!

Many years ago, people did not have rulers or measuring sticks like we do today. So they used whatever they had…and they had hands. So horses are measured in hands. You can do this too! One hand is 4 inches.

So if a horse is 15 hands multiply this by 4. (15 x 4) and you will get 60 inches. And if a horse is 16 hands multiply this number by 4. (16 x 4) and you will get 64 inches.

Now that you know how to do it, you can measure the other horses for yourself. Have fun!

Suffolk Punch

Looking great

Not just another horse: Let's talk about a unique characteristic of the Suffolk Punch. This breed is called a Good Doer. What does that name sound like to you? Are you thinking Do-Gooder?
Not quite! This title really means: Easy Keeper.

In British English it would be Easy Doer. So what does all of this mean? Well, the Suffolk Punch is a horse that can live on just a little bit of food unlike other horses that need a lot of food to eat. Isn't that interesting?

It is more common to find these types of animals (Good Doer) in those who were bred for difficult conditions. Most of the breeds of Ponies fall into this category and in this case the Suffolk Punch.

How can you tell what a Good Doer is?

The first thing is how they gain weight. It tends to be ALL over their body instead of just a part of it. It also gains weight much quicker than other horses and will lose weight much slower than other horses.

This grass is yummy

Characteristics: The Suffolk Punch stands at approximately: 16.1 to 17.2. Do you remember how to find the inches? Then calculate the hands for yourself and you will find the inches!

Weight: 1,900 - 2,000 pounds and up.

These horses have a very distinct color. There are many variations of this color, but it is all the same color. Remember the name? Excellent! It's Chesnut.

This breed may be shorter than others but they have a solid build. This means their body is strong and sturdy. Their neck is strong too and they have a wide back. Look at their feet. They do not have much, if any, feathering on their *fetlocks*.

If you've never heard of this word before it simply means: Ankle. Of course this is not the correct term, but it is a word we can easily understand.

It is also important to note the curiosity in this breed. If they spot something new, they will get closer and check it out for themselves.

I think I see something. Let's jump the fence!

Training: These horses are highly intelligent. The website: *Eagleridgesuffolk.com* calls them: "*Incredibly intelligent*" as part of the outstanding characteristics of the Suffolk Punch. What makes them so smart?

The website notes that the Suffolk Punch is "*well suited to all skill and age levels.*" That's a nice ability, don't you agree? Not all horses are the same and some are too skittish or nervous for unskilled riders. Not the Suffolk Punch!

Once they are properly trained, their good nature, docile temperament and patience make an ideal horse for any rider to try. But this is not the only advantage to the Suffolk Punch. This horse actually tries to understand you. They are also honest and willing to give the best of themselves.

Caution: The Suffolk Punch is a lovable horse, but we have already learned that they come from draft horses. This means they will work themselves to exhaustion or collapse unless they stop to rest. Just like us, these beautiful horses need time to relax and recover their strength. They need time to eat too even if they don't eat that much!

Training: Horses, like most if not all people, like to be respected. The Suffolk Punch is no different. ***EagleRidgeSuffolk.com*** recommends respecting the horse's wishes and getting them to trust you. It also involves getting the horse to want to spend time with you.

There are several ways to do this and *Wikihow* recommends the following steps:

1-*First of all, don't scare the horse*. That means you should not run up or sneak up on them suddenly. This is not a hard concept to understand. For example, do you like it when people run or sneak up on you suddenly? It may scare you when someone does that, right? Then a horse will feel the same way!

2-*Be gentle and talk gently to your horse*. There is no need to yell, shout or talk in a harsh tone to your horse. Again, this idea is not hard to understand. Do you like it when people talk to you gently? Or do you want them to shout and yell at you? Isn't it nicer to treat others kindly and don't you appreciate it when others do the same for you? Your horse will appreciate your kind manner too!

3-*Most horses love to be touched*. So you can show them your feelings through your hands. You can stroke them on the head, massage their neck, hug them, brush them and communicate your affection through gentle fingers. Imagine how happy your horse will be!

4-*Try to spend as much time as you can with your horse*. In any friendship, regular visits are the key! No matter what you have to do, stop by and visit your horse just to remind them that you're there. They will be so happy to see you and the more you spend time with them, the stronger your bond will grow.

5-*A nice reward*. A tasty treat, rub or pat down, yummy food, grooming of whatever other treat you might have in mind, will be a great idea! Do this at the end of the day to let your horse know how much you enjoyed spending time with them.

Royalgrovestables.blogspot.com notes another beautiful attitude of horses. It is their intuition or intuitive nature. This means a horse can *sense* your feelings, emotions and will react on those feelings.

If you are angry, upset, unhappy or grouchy, the horse will sense these negative emotions. This will not help you to get close to them. Instead, they may avoid you. But if you are positive, upbeat and happy to be around them, they will feel this as well. This will draw them to you and you will be able to bond with them!

Chapter 2

A nice, loving hello!

Suffolk Punches' are truly magnificent creatures. But there is still more we can learn about them. And a great place to start is the Suffolk Punch Spectacular & Country Fair. This event is dedicated to showing off these amazing horses.

If you've never heard about it before, this event takes place at the Animal Health Trust at Lanwades Park, UK. It is here that the Suffolk Punch really shines.

The horses are well groomed until their Chesnut coat shines! And their mane and tail is braided with raffia in unique styles. Their owners and presenters are also dressed nicely. The idea is for everyone to look their Sunday best.
There is more than one event and shows like the:

-Suffolk Show
-East England Show
-Royal Norfolk Show
-Royal Show
-Essex Show

These amazing events celebrate the Suffolk Punch and all they mean to the world of horses. During these events you will find stallions, mares, geldings, foals, horse drawn vehicles and wagons.

The members who are part of this group and the Suffolk Horse Society are working very hard to save the Suffolk Punch for future generations!

Hello there!

CURIOUS FACT FOR KIDS:

Horses, like us, have different titles for different stages of life. For example when a horse is born until 6 months of age it is called a *foal*.

Then up to the age of 2 years it is called a *yearling*. If the horse is a male horse it is called a *colt* under the age of 4. When it is older than 4 years it is called a *stallion*. Do you remember what a Stallion is?

Meaning of Terms:

A *stallion* is a: Male horse that can have kids.

A *gelding* is a: Male horse that cannot have kids. (Geldings are usually patient, calm, quiet and well behaved.)

A young female horse or pony is called *filly* and after the age of 4, she is called a *mare*. (Source: *Lessonpaths.com*)

Just resting

Suffolk Punch

A famous Suffolk Punch: In 2014, a Suffolk Punch by the name Achilles finished a very successful show at the Woodbridge Horse Show. He did really well in the events and won the Supreme Champion title to the happiness of his owner. Congratulations Achilles! (Source: ***SuffolkTrustPunch.org***)

Suffolk Punch

Chapter 3

There is no doubt Suffolk Punches' are unique horses! Here are a few additional facts about horses in general you may like to know. (Source: *Onekind.org*)

-A horse can express its emotions in many different ways. It can use its face, eyes and ears to tell you how it feels!

-Horses are great at keeping watch. It is rare to see a herd with everyone snoozing at one time. There is usually one horse standing as a lookout, and his job is to warn the others if danger comes near!

- Avoid standing behind a horse. They have great vision, but there are a couple of blind spots. Can you guess what the back part of the horse is? Yes! It's a blind spot. If the horse gets angry or scared, guess what he may do if you stand directly behind him?

-Horses are great at listening! They can turn their ears in different ways to improve their hearing. If you whisper and say something bad about your horse, they just might hear you!

- Horses can help people get better when they have mental or health problems. This is called: *Equine Assisted Therapy*.

-The Suffolk Punch is known as the oldest type of horse breeds! The male of the horse traces its origins back to a horse called "Crisp's Horse of Ufford."

-A Suffolk Punch starts to work from the early age of 2. As time goes on, this gentle giant continues with heavier workloads. The reason for this is because of the obedience and willing nature of the Suffolk Punch. They are very easy to train and very easy to learn.

-In 2002, in New Bedford, Massachusetts a Suffolk Punch mare gave birth to a beautiful female foal. What makes this birth unique is the following: This baby is the first to be born in a zoo in the United States. Isn't that amazing? (Source: ***Terrificpets.com***)

-On January 3, 2015 the BBC has a very interesting article on the future of the Suffolk Punch. So far there are 170 registered adult breeding females according to the Rare Breeds Survival Trust. Worldwide, there are thought to be approximately 520. However, Clare Barber from the trust said, "*They're one of the few breeds showing small increases in their population, which is very, very positive.*"

Nice snowy day

GENERAL HORSE TIPS FOR KIDS:

If you are able to get a horse, you will need to care for it. So here are some tips you can think about: (Frank Bell- ***Horsewhisperer.com***)

-Your horse's diet is very important. Some horses have very hot blood and some have cooler blood. If your horse is hot blooded, they will need less protein in their diet. The Suffolk Punch is cold blood.

Suffolk Punch

-Learn how to properly discipline your horse. Remember: These animals are very sensitive. Let them know when they are getting too out of control! This can be done with a shhhhh noise or a firm tone to let them know who is in control.

-If the horse's head is high it means your horse is not relaxed. They may be uptight. If their head if low they are relaxed. Try to ensure your horse is always relaxed. This will help them feel good and both of you will enjoy the ride.

-Horses love to get your tender rubs and soft patting. Things like rubbing their ears, nose, eyes and mouth is great. And if you massage it, it's even better!

-If a horse is trained really well, he or she will invite YOU for a ride. You should be looking for the invitation! Then you know you will enjoy an awesome ride.

-Your horse can sense your moods and behavior. If you are confident your horse will be confident too!

-You should feed your horse from a bucket and not your hand. (This is the recommendation, but I feel it is better to feed them with your hand from time to time! It seems to generate more trust and respect, but that is just my humble opinion on the subject. What do you think?)

INTERESTING FACT FOR KIDS

Do you know the scientific name for horses? They are called Equines which comes from the Latin word meaning Equus Caballus. Can you think of any other creature that looks like a horse? Did you think of a donkey? Maybe a Zebra? What about a mule? These are also related to the Equus Caballus.

Horses can live for many years. Some for 30 years and in some cases 40 years or more! Ponies can live for a very long time too. But if you want to know how old they are you need to look into the horse's mouth! Have you heard of this practice before? Usually the approximate age of a horse is estimated based on the incisors, upper and lower in the mouth. What is that? The teeth!

Can you tell how old you are by looking at your teeth? (Source: *Lessonpaths.com*)

Conclusion

Hello everyone!

In conclusion: Horses are beautiful creatures, and the Suffolk Punch is no exception. This "gentle giant" is a magnificent horse and there are many things we can still learn about them. Just like any other creature, they have feelings, emotions and need to be treated with love, kindness and respect.

They are strong, faithful, loyal and willing to work hard. They are also ready to go the "extra" mile if you want them to. Why don't you take the time to learn a little bit more about them? You may be amazed at what you discover. If you don't know where to look, ask your teacher, a parent or guardian to help you. Choose something you really like about this horse and learn a bit more about it.

It is true that there is not a lot of information about these beautiful creatures available, but there is still quite a bit of find. I hope this book has taught you just how wonderful all of earth's creatures are and how each one can impact our life in amazing ways! Suffolk Punches' like all other creatures are truly one of nature's magnificent wonders!

Suffolk Punch

Author Bio

K. Bennett loves to write for both children and adults. Many different subjects are interesting to develop, but writing for children is special to her heart.

Her favorite pastimes include reading, traveling and discovering new things. Each of these activities helps to fuel her imagination and acts like a blank canvas waiting for more stories.

She is intrigued with fantasy elements like hidden worlds and faraway lands. Basically anything that gets her imagination soaring to new heights!

Her writing credits include children books online, short stories for online magazines, and two novellas listed at Amazon.com

Our books are available at

1. Amazon.com

2. Barnes and Noble

3. Itunes

4. Kobo

5. Smashwords

6. Google Play Books

Suffolk Punch

This book is published by

JD-Biz Corp

P O Box 374

Mendon, Utah 84325

http://www.jd-biz.com/

Read more books from John Davidson

Amazon.com Author Link

Suffolk Punch

www.ingramcontent.com/pod-product-compliance
Lightning Source LLC
Chambersburg PA
CBHW050925290526
45792CB00002B/887